PRAYING YOUR CHURCH INTO HER GLORIOUS DESTINY

A Practical Guide to Becoming The Bride of Christ

AMELDA THOMAS-JONES

Praying Your Church Into Her Glorious Destiny

By
AMELDA THOMAS-JONES

COPYRIGHT © 2010 by
F.A.I.T.H. Clarion Call Publications
P.O. Box 1213
O'Fallon, IL 62269

First Printing, September 2009
Second Printing, July 2010

ISBN: 978-0-615-38106-0
Library of Congress Control Number: 2010932553

Printed in the United States of America

<u>Dedication</u>

I dedicate this book to my Lord Jesus Christ, the One who is positioning and preparing His Bride for her glorious destiny.

I also dedicate this book to my grandmother, Cordillia Salomon. In fact, everything I write on prayer I dedicate to her. She groomed my life even when not wanting her to, but she was diligent to do so. I consider her to be the best intercessor I have ever known. She was a woman of integrity and hard working with an intimate relationship with the Father, the Son, and the Holy Ghost. She walked, talked, and communed with them as if they were right there in front of her. I am blessed to have been called by my grandmother a fourth generation intercessor. We prayer walked before it was a popular thing to do. I loved her with all my heart.

<u>Acknowledgments</u>

First and foremost I thank the Lord for His insight and the Holy Spirit for bringing everything to memory to be able to impart this book into you.

Special thanks to my beloved children Ellis E. Jones, and Leon and Marjorie Hall whose encouragement in recalling the stories prompted me to write this book.

Special thanks to Delores H. Harris, F.A.I.T.H. Executive Minister; Dagne Moore-Joy, Executive Assistant to my Bishop, Geoffrey V. Dudley, Sr., D.Min. (F.A.I.T.H.'s covering); and Greg and Karen Fry for their tireless support and encouragement in editing this work of the Lord.

Table of Contents

Introduction

The writing of this book is intentional. My main purpose is to leave it as a gift, a legacy, for generations to come. These coming generations are not my "tomorrow" – they are my "today." I am compelled of the Lord to train them in hearing and responding to the still small voice of God – a discipline that has spanned the ages and flows out of an intimate relationship with our loving Father God. It is imperative for the intercessor and person of prayer to have this intimate relationship with God because His voice is the only voice we should respond to in preparing the Church for His glorious return.

My mandate from God is to prepare the Church to meet her destiny. Christ will return. He expects the Church to be a certain way: *"...not having spot or wrinkle or any such thing,..." (Ephesians 5:27)*

At age nine, my grandmother mentored and coached me in the ways of intercessory prayer. We never prayed without the Bible open; as God would say something to her, she would go to the Bible and start praying what she was reading. She also taught me how to hear and respond to the voice of God even as Eli did for Samuel.

> *Now the boy Samuel ministered to the LORD before Eli. And the word of the LORD was rare in those days; there was no widespread revelation ... and while Samuel was lying down, that the LORD called Samuel. And he answered, "Here I am!" So he ran to Eli and said, "Here I am, for you called me." And he said, "I did not call; lie down again." And he went and lay down. Then the LORD called yet again, "Samuel!"*

*So Samuel arose and went to Eli, and said, "Here I am, for you called me." He answered, "I did not call, my son; lie down again." (Now Samuel did not yet know the LORD, nor was the word of the LORD yet revealed to him). And the LORD called Samuel again the third time. So he arose and went to Eli, and said, "Here I am, for you did call me." Then Eli perceived that the LORD had called the boy. Therefore Eli said to Samuel, "Go, lie down; and it shall be, if He calls you, that you must say, 'Speak, LORD, for Your servant hears.'" So Samuel went and lay down in his place. Now the LORD came and stood and called as at other times, "Samuel! Samuel!" And Samuel answered, "**Speak, for Your servant hears**." Then the LORD said to Samuel: "Behold, I will do something in Israel at which both ears of everyone who hears it will tingle." (1 Samuel 3:1-11)*

Rebellious as I may have been, I have never forgotten the tutelage of my grandmother through the years. Today I can still hear the soft voice of my Lord. It is His voice that inspires and directs my prayers – a discipline taught to me by my grandmother. This legacy of hearing and praying the voice of God I have instilled in my biological children and pray that it would now be instilled in you through the reading of this book.

The Lord is calling the Church to be proactive and disciplined in prayer. This book will focus on four specific areas of how to pray your church into *"Her Glorious Destiny:"*

1) Praying for Your Church
2) Praying in the Prayer Room
3) Praying for God's Vision
4) The Intercessor's Response

How to Use This Book

This is an interactive book which highlights many truths from God's Word. Each shaded box in the text [_____] represents a Scripture you are to research and annotate into the space provided. Each Scriptural reference can then be verified in the Appendix at the back of the book.

Take Selah moments. Pause and meditate on what you have read and allow the Holy Spirit to speak and lead you. Slow down and listen for the still small voice of God. Then capture the revelations through journaling in the space provided at the end of each chapter.

This book is meant to be used as a tool as we *"contend earnestly for the faith." (Jude 3)* My prayer is that this book will equip and encourage you in *"Praying Your Church Into Her Glorious Destiny."*

The following Scripture is the foundational truth to this transforming call to the Church:

> *"...that He might sanctify and cleanse her*
> *with the washing of water by the word,*
> *that He might present her to Himself*
> ***a glorious church**, not having spot or wrinkle*
> *or any such thing, but that she should be*
> *holy and without blemish."*
> *Ephesians 5:26-27*

Now is the time for generations of praying children, youth, adults, and seniors to rise up and contend together for the glorious destiny of the Church. We serve a God of generations: the God of Abraham, Isaac, and Jacob. To the Builders (the Abrahams) and the

Baby Boomers (the Isaacs), the Lord would have me encourage you. We are the generations on whose shoulders the coming generations, our "todays," will stand; we are to be the foundation from which this generation will know their God. *"This is Jacob, the generation of those who seek Him, who seek Your face."* *(Psalm 24:6)*

We are to leave them a godly inheritance. It is from this inheritance, and our example, they will become the shoulders to those following them to stand upon to know and serve their God.

Now, may the Church arise in newfound power as the generations prayerfully unite, responding to the voice of God to move into her finest hour, *"Her Glorious Destiny"* – to become the Bride of Christ!

Section I

Praying for Your Church

"...that He might sanctify and cleanse her
with the washing of water by the word,
that He might present her to Himself
a glorious church, not having spot or wrinkle
or any such thing, but that she should be
holy and without blemish."
Ephesians 5:26-27

Chapter 1

Who is Called to Pray?

You are called, I am called. We are <u>all</u> called to pray. Prayer is one of the most powerful vehicles the Church has in preparing for the return of Jesus Christ.

The Bible states to *"...pray without ceasing."*[1] [_____] Once we, as individuals, accept our role and are fully prepared, it is our individual and corporate responsibility to be a praying church. Then the praying church becomes a powerful living organism armed with the Word of God, and the *"gates of Hades shall not prevail against it."*[2] [_____]

We must stand fast knowing this is not just the role of the intercessor. This is the role of every member of the Church. Special gifts do not preclude you and me from praying. God has called each born again believer to this post of prayer. We cannot relegate it only to a few. We are ALL called. The Scripture makes it clear *"...that men always ought to pray."*[3] [_____] Even though the Scripture calls all of us to pray, *"The heart is deceitful above all things, and desperately wicked; who can know it?"*[4] [_____] Hence, the preparation of our heart is important. God needs to prepare our hearts for service to Him. As we allow Him to do that, our prayers will fortify our church and we become a praying church.

The Praying Church
- **A praying church** is alive. It knows it is not only operating when prayer is called; it is a way of life and releases transformational change.

- A **praying church** is a soul winning, living, and breathing organism. It is in *"Him we live and move and have our being,"*[5] [_____]
- A **praying church** brings *"all their tithes"*[6] [_____] into the Church.
- A **praying church** has *"each one give as he purposes in his heart."*[7] [_____]
- A **praying church** gives of their tithes, offerings, and time where they are fed.
- A **praying church** knows that giving to your church is your responsibility.
- A **praying church** is an orderly church: timely, loving, helpful, *"...all things are done decently and in order."*[8] [_____]
- A **praying church** is powerful. *"The effectual fervent prayer of a righteous man avails much."*[9] [_____]
- A **praying church** is intentionally taught. In the daily reading of God's Word, know it goes hand in hand with prayer. These two together cause us to want to be a praying church. *"Be diligent to present yourself approved to God, a worker who does not need to be ashamed, rightly dividing the word of truth."*[10] [_____]
- A **praying church** is in covenant relationship. When we are in covenant with God and one another, the vision to pray for our church becomes natural. It's relational. *"For where two or three are gathered together in My name, I am there in the midst of them."*[11] [_____]
- A **praying church** is *"...to contend earnestly for the faith..."*[12] [_____]
- A **praying church** prays in the name of Jesus. *"And whatever you ask in My name, that I will do..."*[13] [_____]

- **A praying church** fulfills the commandment to *"love one another."*[14] [   ]
- **A praying church** contends for the protection of the unborn.
- **A praying church** cares for one another.
- **A praying church** does not tolerate injustice.
- **A praying church** seeks God for His Kingdom to come and His *"...will be done on earth as it is in heaven."*[15] [   ]
- **A praying church** has a strong devotional lifestyle; a lifestyle that rules their lives and permeates into their church, home, marketplace, and beyond.
- **A praying church** is comprised of individuals with a lifestyle of prayer who do not have to be coerced to enter into prayer.

A church becomes a praying church when the call to pray is obeyed. Then, our prayers begin to flow from the very heart of God - prayers to release the Church into *"Her Glorious Destiny."*

Selah Moments (pause and meditate) – journal personal reflections from the Lord:

_____

_____

_____

_____

_____

_____

_____

_____

Chapter 2

Why Pray?

Every church has its' own individual fingerprint, or DNA, from the Lord. It is what makes that church unique; just like no two snowflakes are alike, there are no two churches alike. They may look similar; however, there is that "something" that they are known for that makes them unique, a one of a kind. It is what God has created them to be so they can accomplish what God has called them to do. Do you know the uniqueness and God's vision for your church?

If so, every one of us should be able to pray. God has called us, His Body, to always pray. Therefore, wanting to pray for a Glorious Church should be our delight knowing He is returning for a church *"not having spot, or wrinkle, or any such thing; but that it should be holy and without blemish."* [16] [_____]

Passion for Prayer

Prayer is my passion. I've been at this for awhile. Whenever I think of the Lord's return and the condition of the Church, I ask myself the question, "Why isn't the Church praying more?" Don't we realize it is one of the foremost ways we can prepare the Church for His return?

Since 1971, I would find people to pray with. In 1977 while stationed at Howard Air Force Base (AFB) in Panama, I formally started prayer groups wherever we would travel from base to base. After leaving Ramstein AFB in Germany in 1983, I moved to Scott AFB in Illinois. The first thing I did at the Chapel was to start a

17

prayer group called, "Father Answers Intercessors Travailing in Holiness" (F.A.I.T.H.) to pray for the Armed Forces personnel and their families.

Praying for the Armed Forces personnel and their families by then was innate. The Lord said to me, "I have called F.A.I.T.H. as an Emissary of Intercession for the Department of Defense and their families." It was at that time the Lord illuminated to me, "It was through the Armed Forces 'I' send you along with your family to Europe, the Pacific, the Continental U.S., Alaska, and beyond." Prayer seemed to go wherever I went.

It was at Scott AFB I knew God was calling people of prayer. The group was very strong with people praying Sunday mornings from 6:00 to 7:00. After we left Scott AFB, F.A.I.T.H. continued and my passion for prayer heightened with subsequent military assignments. To this present day, my passion continues.

Prayer should be purposeful in the Church. The intent is to unite our hearts as we gather. Prayer causes us to focus on the things of God. Prayer opens our heart to the purpose of God and is a guiding force as the Holy Spirit teaches and leads us *"into all truth."* [17] [_____]

Reasons to Pray
The question I am most frequently asked while conducting Prayer Seminars/Workshops is, "Why pray?" I believe the church who prays is a disciplined church. Prayer brings our focus into the place God would have us to be in His affairs. I also believe a church that does not see prayer as a priority is only another social entity. For that matter, any area or ministry of a church that

does not open and close with prayer, I believe, does not reverence the Lord.

Prayer in the Church is one of the ways we can ask the Lord to lead and empower us. The Church should be preparing for soul winning revival and discipleship to break out in every area of our churches.

The following are foundational reasons to pray:
- **Why pray?** Praying is communicating with God. *"...let your requests be made known God."*[18] [_____]
- **Why pray?** Praying the vision God gave the leader of the church (or country, mission, ministry) brings it into existence.
- **Why pray?** Prayer is seeking and hearing the voice of God for instruction and direction as David did as he *"...inquired of the LORD, saying, 'Shall I pursue this troop? Shall I overtake them?'"*[19] [_____]
- **Why pray?** Prayer is receiving specific instruction from the Lord as we inquire of Him. *"And God answered David, 'Pursue, for you shall surely overtake them and without fail recover all.'"*[20] [_____]
- **Why pray?** Prayer is having the confidence that God will do what He said He will do. *"God is not a man, that He should lie, nor a son of man, that He should repent."*[21] [_____]
- **Why pray?** Prayer is a means of seeking and finding God. *"And you will seek Me and find Me, when you search for Me with all your heart."*[22] [_____]
- **Why pray?** Prayer is a mandate from God. *"I desire therefore that the men pray everywhere, lifting up holy hands, without wrath and doubting;"*[23] [_____]

- **Why pray?** Prayer is our response to God's desire for us to stand in the gap. *"So I sought for a man among them who would make a wall, and stand in the gap before Me on behalf of the land, that I should not destroy it; but I found no one."* [24] [_____]

- **Why pray?** Prayer leads to godliness and reverence. *"Therefore I exhort first of all that supplications, prayers, intercessions, and giving of thanks be made for all men, for kings and all who are in authority, that we may lead a quiet and peaceable life in all godliness and reverence."* [25] [_____]

- **Why pray?** Prayer is a response to God's call to repentance so He can respond appropriately as we turn from ourselves to Him. Keeping in mind, it is conditional. God said: *"If My people who are called by My name will humble themselves, and pray and seek My face, and turn from their wicked ways, then I will hear from heaven, and will forgive their sin and heal their land."* [26] [_____]

Selah Moments (pause and meditate) – journal personal reflections from the Lord:

_____

_____

_____

_____

_____

_____

_____

_____

Chapter 3

Words of Wisdom
To Those Who Pray

DROP THE BAGGAGE! The successful intercessors and people of prayer are those who are navigating through life living without a spirit of offense and following this Scripture:

"Brethren, I do not count myself to have apprehended;
but one thing I do, forgetting
those things which are behind and reaching forward to
those things which are ahead,
I press toward the goal for the prize of the
upward call of God in Christ Jesus."
Philippians 3:13-14

This is a **must** in *"Praying Your Church into Her Glorious Destiny."* We must be *"looking unto Jesus, the author and finisher of our faith."* [27] [_____] We must also forgive *"...one another, even as God in Christ forgave you."* [28] [_____] It is imperative!

Walk in Purity
Basic Prayer 101 must be done only one way: with *"clean hands and a pure heart"* [29] [_____] – bottom line! It is time that we as intercessors and people of prayer stop fooling ourselves. We cannot drink communion having an aught against our brothers and/or sisters fully knowing the schemes and plots we are having in our heart against one another. Get up! Get it right – it is not a bad thing to ask people to forgive you! Do you not know *"...the Lord looks at the heart."* [30] [_____]

Do you not realize, *"Do not be deceived, God is not mocked."*[31] [_____]

Keep a pure heart. Do not harbor hate in your heart for those who have manipulated or said all manner of evil against you. Remember your purpose. People have tried to manipulate me at the altar. I have also had those who lied about me maliciously. In any case, I asked their forgiveness even if I was not in the wrong. We must practice *"...forgiving one another, even as God in Christ forgave you."*[32] [_____]

The intercessor and person of prayer must practice Matthew 18 at all times. Their heart motivation must be right toward one another. Never become a stumbling block or ingratiate yourself. The Scripture says, *"If your hand or foot causes you to sin, cut it off and cast it from you."*[33] [_____] This does not mean literally cut it off. It is talking about spiritual surgery, mortifying the flesh (your will; your willpower; turning areas over to the Lord and asking Him to help you; your way of thinking as opposed to God's way) and self-denial to obtain eternal life.

Stay Focused
Keep in mind the winning of souls is very dear to the Lord and thus it should be a priority in our prayers. *"For the Son of Man has come to save that which was lost."*[34] [_____]

Seek people to pray with who will help you stand on the Word of God. *"For where two or three are gathered together in My name, I am there in the midst of them."*[35] [_____]

Ask God to give you a mentor; not a "yes" person, but one who will mentor you with love and still be able to make the tough calls from the LORD.

Other Considerations
Always be humble. Be the intercessor and person of prayer who will fall on their faces, humbling themselves before God first. Ask Him for His battle plan, His strategy, and a Word for your situation.

Stay encouraged even when there are not throngs of people in the prayer ministry. Practice connecting with the Lord who "...always lives to make intercession..."[36] [   ]

Do not exceed your gifting. You cannot take people where you have never been, and/or lead them in areas in which you are unfamiliar. Continue to grow and invest in your gift. Be teachable. Do you know what happens when "the blind leads the blind."[37] [   ] "Therefore, brethren, be even more diligent to make your call and election sure,..."[38] [   ] Be all that God created you to be in the ministry of prayer.

Selah Moments (pause and meditate) – journal personal reflections from the Lord:

_____

_____

_____

_____

_____

_____

_____

Chapter 4

The Intercessor's Role

I have often wondered why, of all the gifts the Lord gave the Church, the only one He went to heaven to do is the ministry of intercession. Have you not wondered that also? *"...He always lives to make intercession..."* [39]
[_____]

The intercessor, while praying their *"Church into Her Glorious Destiny,"* should know the vision of their church; keeping in mind there is one visionary, the Senior Pastor. And if your church has a Prayer Pastor, this is the person to keep God's vision alive for new people to pray into.

What is an Intercessor?
I heard the word intercession before I could spell the word. There are some who say to me, "I'm not an intercessor" or "How do I know I'm an intercessor?" My response is always the same: "Pray, ask the Holy Spirit to lead you. He will; you will not have to conjure up anything." In Ezekiel it says, the Lord *"sought for a man among them who would...stand in the gap...; but I found no one."* [40] [_____] If He sought for someone to pray and make up the hedge, then He will provide for you how to pray.

Know that intercessory prayer is the unseen support structure. Each time I look at the support beams and metal rods of a new building going up, I'll say to myself, "That's the intercessor or person of prayer; the area no one sees." It is the inner structure of a new building that must pass rigorous inspections to see if it will stand the

25

test of time. And it is the same for intercessors. The intercessor must be flexible like the earthquake-proofed buildings – bend under pressure, but do not break!

There are many people standing on the shoulders of intercessors and people of prayer. The weight of the call sometimes will make the intercessor want to break; but they are connected with the chief intercessor, Jesus Christ, who will pray them through.

Having said that, realize this is vital. Trust me. You do not have to be seen or heard by man to be effective. When it is all said and done, it is the motivation of your heart that will be in question. If God wants you to be known, you will be. *"A man's gift makes room for him, and brings him before great men."* [41] [_____]

Character of an Intercessor
Intercessors, people of prayer, and the whole Body of Christ should continually pursue *"clean hands and a pure heart"* [42] [_____] before God. Don't seek the approval of man.

Let's settle a long-standing dispute that I have heard in churches for some time. People would make this statement to me, "I am not an intercessor" or "I am an intercessor." The one who says, "I am not an intercessor" at times may feel insignificant or inferior. That person may even be afraid; intimidated to pray where others may hear them. There may be occasions when others lord over the one who already is feeling unqualified to pray. This is wrong. Being an intercessor does not give us a license above others. Instead, we should always encourage and edify those we pray with.

26

Could it be that while looking for the intercessors to make up the hedge, God could not find one because they were having arguments – comparing themselves and lording over the people of God? Do not compare yourselves. Greatness is not how you lord over the people of God. Greatness comes out of a servants' heart. Your effectiveness in *"Praying Your Church into Her Glorious Destiny"* comes from a spirit of humility. *"...he who is greatest among you, let him be as the younger, and he who governs as he who serves."* [43] [_____]

We intercessors need not to fight amongst ourselves. If you have a dispute against your brother, settle it among yourselves. *"If he hears you, you have gained your brother."* [44] [_____] *"But if he will not hear, take with you one or two more, that 'by the mouth of two or three witnesses every word may be established.'"* [45] [_____] Keep no animosity or spirit of offense in your heart against each other; *"forgiving one another, just as God in Christ also forgave you."* [46] [_____]

In the spiritual kingdom, humility and service enjoin a servant's heart. Intercessors and people of prayer should be quick to repent and ask for forgiveness, *"...endeavoring to keep the unity of the Spirit in the bond of peace."* [47] [_____]

Everyone is called to pray our churches into her glorious destiny, *"that He might sanctify and cleanse her with the washing of water by the word, that He might present her to Himself a glorious church, not having spot or wrinkle or any such thing, but that she should be holy and without blemish."* [48] [_____] This Scripture is not just for us to pray for the Church; but it has personal application for us, the intercessor and people of prayer.

Come before God clean. *"Be holy, for I am holy."* [49]
[_____] There should be no power struggle in
the Body of Christ. We have a world to be praying for to
come to the knowledge of God. Keep in mind that *"we
do not wrestle against flesh and blood."* [50] [_____]
People of God should come clean. *"If we confess our
sins..."* [51] [_____]

Take the Word of God: *"Put on the whole armor of
God"* [52] [_____] while we *"contend earnestly for
the faith."* [53] [_____] Also, *"...do not worry about
how or what you should speak"* [54] [_____]; the
Lord will equip you to pray.

Your confidence is in Jesus Christ. He will build your
character. Be a team player. Never allow your mouth to
cause you to sin. While others are praying, you come in
the power of agreement in the name of Jesus. You do
not have to have the last word in prayer or pray
everything.

Practical Guidelines for an Intercessor
The following are guidelines for fulfilling the role of an
intercessor:
• Do not seek or want one-on-one time with the
  pastor or key leaders for personal favor.
• Do not seek recognition.
• Do not be offended if not recognized.
• Do not ingratiate yourself with others in order to
  gain attention, position, status, favor, or power.
• Speak the truth in love at all times.
• *"Be kindly affectionate to one another."* [55] [_____]
• Do not be envious or jealous of another person's
  position.

- Do not compromise yourself with God or lie to gain favor. What you have done in secret, your heavenly Father knows how to reward you openly, if He chooses. *"...pray to your Father...; and your Father who sees in secret will reward you openly."* [56]
  [＿＿＿＿＿＿＿]
- Do not be prideful about sharing the victories God used you to pray in.
- Be strong, you *"shall not be afraid of the terror by night or the arrow that flies by day."* [57]
  [＿＿＿＿＿＿＿]
- Pray for the Godhead to guide you.

Having said all of the this, let us take hold of the promises of God with full assurance; knowing we are co-laboring in intercession with the Lord, Who forever lives to make intercession for us. Together we are preparing His Church for His return which is *"Her Glorious Destiny!"*

Selah Moments (pause and meditate)   journal personal reflections from the Lord:

_____
_____
_____
_____
_____
_____
_____
_____

Section II

Praying in the Prayer Room

*"...that He might sanctify and cleanse her
with the washing of water by the word,
that He might present her to Himself
a glorious church, not having spot or wrinkle
or any such thing, but that she should be
holy and without blemish."*
Ephesians 5:26-27

Chapter 5

Purpose of the Prayer Room

The sole purpose of the Prayer Room is to pray for God's Word to go forth and pierce the hearts of men through the whole worship experience.

The Prayer Room is not the place to pray for our needs; neither is its intent to hold conversation and get caught up on the latest gossip in the church; nor get information we may have missed. We are there to pray in unity for God's purposes to come forth in the service.

In setting up a Prayer Room, I encourage you to pray. First, seek the Lord to give you discernment so you can receive the things of God. Second, know the uniqueness of the spiritual fingerprint and God's vision for your church. Third, ask the Lord for intercessors and people of prayer to pray for the prayer assignment. Fourthly, ask the Lord for a place to pray.

I believe the Prayer Room should be a well-known place, purposefully designated for praying individuals. As the worship service is in progress, they pray God's will to be in their church – from the parking lot to the benediction. Persons in the Prayer Room must remain focused and avoid confusion at all costs.

There are four key considerations regarding the Prayer Room: 1) find a consistent location; 2) determine when to pray; 3) communicate expectations; and 4) establish decorum.

1) **Find a consistent location:**   Intercessors and persons of prayer should know the Prayer Room's exact location beforehand. It should not be changed at the last minute without their prior knowledge.

2) **Determine when to pray:** The time is during the services. For each worship service, there should be at least two people of the same gender scheduled. For any other prayer assignments using the Prayer Room, secure the time and be consistent: know the purpose, remain focused, and pray in the name of Jesus.

3) **Communicate expectations:** Have clearly defined expectations that are understood. Those praying must have a willingness to pray and not gossip. They should be in the Prayer Room at least fifteen minutes prior to prayer time clothed in integrity and equipped with their Bible, bottled drinking water, and breath mints.

4) **Establish decorum:** The Prayer Room has a decorum of good manners, good behavior, modesty, respectability, correctness, demureness, etiquette, and restraints which will not be abandoned! The decorum of the intercessor or person of prayer in the Prayer Room should be one devoted to the reading of the Word, one who has an intimate relationship with the Godhead, and one who is in love with the Lord since *"We love Him because He first loved us."*[58] [＿＿＿＿＿＿]

There are specific types of prayer that should be covered from the Prayer Room during every worship service. These include, but are not limited to, the following:
* **Praise the Lord:** Start with adorations, praise, and thanksgiving.

- **Pray for direction:** Ask the Lord to speak giving you direction to pray.
- **Pray against hindrances:** Ask the Lord to remove all hindrances that would keep anyone from receiving and responding to the preached/taught Word of God in the house! God promises that His Word *"shall not return to Me void."*[59] [_____]
- **Pray for fruit:** That everyone involved in the worship service would be *"...fruitful in every good work and increasing in the knowledge of God;"*[60] [_____]
- **Pray for salvation:** People, *"do not harden your heart"*[61] [_____] and respond to the Word.
- **Pray for deliverance:** That people would have their hearts open to the truth, *"...and the truth shall make you free."*[62] [_____]
- **Pray for healing:** That people would come, be healed and set free. *"Therefore if the Son makes you free, you shall be free indeed."*[63] [_____]
- **Pray for peace:** That people would find peace, *"...that He might reconcile them both back to God..."*[64] [_____]
- **Pray for God's will:** Petition God for the individual needs of the people including jobs, home, and family. *"Your Kingdom come, Your will be done on earth as it is in heaven."*[65] [_____]
- **Pray for signs and wonders:** *"And these signs will follow those who believe: In My name they will..."*[66] [_____]
- **Pray with confidence:** *"Now this is the confidence that we have in Him, that if we ask anything according to His will, He hears us. And if we know that He hears us, whatever we ask, we know that we have the petitions that we have asked of Him."*[67] [_____]

What a blessing to partner with God, our heavenly Father, in the ministry of prayer. This we can do with full assurance knowing God will use our prayer time in the Prayer Room to release our church into *"Her Glorious Destiny!"*

Selah Moments (pause and meditate) – journal personal reflections from the Lord:

_____

_____

_____

_____

_____

_____

_____

Chapter 6

Who Should Be in the Prayer Room?

Each person in the Prayer Room should be there to pray for God's purposes to be fulfilled through the worship service.

The Prayer Pastor (or member of the clergy, if the church doesn't have a Prayer Pastor), or their designee, is the first line of defense for authorizing who is to pray in the Prayer Room.

Intercession During the Worship Service
Everyone with a desire to pray for your church should have access to the Prayer Room once they are trained on the protocol and expectations of praying in the Prayer Room.

There should be regularly scheduled prayer teams for each service made up of a minimum of two to three individuals of the same gender.

Also, every church ministry should have someone praying in the Prayer Room to specifically cover that ministry.

Ministry After the Worship Service
Only trained clergy should pray for people when brought to the Prayer Room after responding to the preached Word. The non-clergy, who were assigned to be in the Prayer Room, should step aside, yet continue

to pray as the clergy and their designee take over in ministry.

Other Times of Prayer
Praying in the Prayer Room is not an affirmation you are called to the Clergy. We are all called to pray. Each prayer assignment for the Prayer Room should be scheduled through the clergy-designated person and each person praying should be notified in advance.

Preparing to Pray
Whenever you go to the Prayer Room, your sins should have been taken care of prior to leaving your home; or, at least, get it done while on your way to church. *"Search me, O God, and know my heart."* [68]
[_____]

Come prepared with *"...clean hands and a pure heart,"* [69]
[_____] so you can hear from God and pray His heart for the service.

Don't be late. Being late is not fashionable – it is disrespectful! Not showing up without making arrangements for a replacement shows lack of integrity; not to man, but to God!!

If you should find yourself the only one in the Prayer Room praying, know that you are not alone. You have the Chief Intercessor in agreement with you on behalf of the service! This is not a license for you not to show up and partner on your designated Sunday. Rather, it is to serve as an encouragement that the Lord *"...will never leave you nor forsake you."* [70] [_____] However, there are circumstances beyond our control that can cause us not to be in the Prayer Room. Always alert the

Prayer Pastor, or his/her designee, if you are not able to fulfill your assignment.

Now is the Time to Pray

It is a blessing to be standing in prayer for whatever service we are called to pray for. Just imagine the power of connecting with other believers in prayer. Can you sense the connection between you and the One who forever lives to make intercession for the saints?

You are trained. Your heart is prepared. Your love for the work of God is proof He has equipped you. Come with confidence into the Prayer Room to pray your church into *"Her Glorious Destiny."*

Selah Moments (pause and meditate) – journal personal reflections from the Lord:

_____

_____

_____

_____

_____

_____

_____

Chapter 7

What to Pray for in the Prayer Room

After an experience of praying through the seven churches of Asia Minor (Turkey), I am convinced that praying the will of God, as revealed in Revelation 2 and 3, will bless your church. Pray from the perspective of the Word spoken to each of these churches: *"He who has an ear, let him hear what the Spirit says to the churches."* [71] [_____]

When you pray through the prayers below, hopefully it will help you in praying for your own church to possess these godly attributes – moving her closer to *"Her Glorious Destiny."*

- **Pray your church** will be loving, not loveless (Revelation 2:1-7).
- **Pray your church** will stand in the face of persecution, not shrink back (Revelation 2:8-11).
- **Pray your church** will walk with integrity, not compromising (Revelation 2:12-17).
- **Pray your church** will be righteous, not corrupt (Revelation 2:18-29).
- **Pray your church** will be alive, not dead (Revelation 3:1-6).
- **Pray your church** will be faithful, not disobedient (Revelation 3:7-13).
- **Pray your church** will be passionate, not lukewarm (Revelation 3:14-22).

Pray for the Worship Service

Pray the Holy Spirit will convict hearts so that He may sanctify and cleanse each person in the worship service with the washing of water through the preached Word. Pray that He might present each person to Himself, a glorious church, not having spot or blemish.

While in the Prayer Room, intercessors or people of prayer should be sensitive to the Holy Spirit to petition the Lord on behalf of those ministering and those seated in the pews.

Prayer Protocol

The following is a prayer protocol that covers the five areas of the worship service. These areas are used by the Lord to bring people to Himself: 1) welcome; 2) worship; 3) word; 4) witness; and 5) workers.

Each church should have a prayer protocol, similar to this one, established by the Senior Pastor, the Prayer Pastor, or the designee for the Prayer Room. Be trained and familiar with the prayer protocol prior to praying in the Prayer Room.

Always pray the Word for each element of the worship service. Keep in mind, "God's Word" should always be used as our guiding Light for intercessory prayer. His *"word is a lamp to my feet and a light to my path."* [72]
[_____]

1) **Welcome:** A welcoming church is a warm church. Start praying before you leave home for the ministries who will be seen first by those arriving for the worship service. Pray each church attendee will feel welcomed.

"...with loving-kindness I have drawn you."[73] [_____]
Know it is the Spirit who has drawn them as He did you.

If your church has a parking lot ministry, this is the first ministry that people see. It is also the first opportunity to welcome and release God's blessing over them. Pray for those in the parking lot ministry, especially during inclement weather that they would be warm and inviting to those arriving. Also, pray for the greeters and ushers as they welcome people into your building and the Sanctuary.

Even when I am not on duty in the Prayer Room, I have made it a practice to start praying Saturday and while I'm preparing for church on Sunday morning for the church attendees, that they would feel welcomed. People should always feel welcomed whenever they enter into the House of the Lord.

2) **Worship:** Praise teams and praise dancers prepare and lead the congregation into the presence of God. Pray the worship is so high the glory of God will fill the Sanctuary. Know the various elements involved in worship as it applies to the church and pray for them. Keep in mind, the Father is seeking those to worship Him *"in spirit and in truth."*[74] [_____] Therefore, we should come prepared to worship Him with all our hearts.

Worshippers are the beacon that draws one into the presence of the Lord. Whenever the heart of the worshipper is prepared in advance to lead worship, we are drawn to the spiritual Light of His presence as moths are drawn to the natural light. Pray for the worshippers to be prepared with clean hands and a pure heart so the

Lord can use them mightily in drawing people to Himself.

Worshippers also prepare the hearts of the people to hear and receive the Word. Pray for the worshippers to go forth plowing the ground and preparing the soil of the heart for the Word that will follow.

An important part of worship and coming before the Lord is to *"bring an offering"*[75] [_____], our first fruits and tithes. Pray for the offering and that it would be given out of a pure heart, *"...for God loves a cheerful giver."*[76] [_____]

3) **Word:** The Word of God is powerful. He promises that *"...it shall not return to Me void, but it shall accomplish what I please..."*[77] [_____] God is sending His Word to the hearts of men to save, heal, deliver, and set free. *"Your word is a lamp unto my feet and a light unto my path."*[78] [_____] *"Your word I have hidden in my heart, that I might not sin against You."*[79] [_____] *"The entrance of Your words gives light; it gives understanding to the simple."*[80] [_____] Pray that the preaching of the Word is *"...not with persuasive words of human wisdom, but in demonstration of the Spirit and of power, that your faith should not be in the wisdom of men but in the power of God."*[81] [_____]

4) **Witness:** In the Prayer Room we are praying for the ones the Lord has brought to church. Pray they will respond to the Word as it was ministered from the "welcome" to the "Word!" *"Behold, I stand at the door and knock."*[82] [_____] *"...and you shall be witnesses to Me..."*[83] [_____]

5) Workers: When I say workers, I am not only talking about the paid staff. Pray for the volunteers who serve, including those administrators who will take the information from the ones who responded to the altar call. We are calling for prayers for all who labor amongst us. We are to know them and, when possible, call them by name. Pray the Father will meet every need they and their families might have.

Pray for a community response. Pray that those who respond to the Word will be discipled so they will become "fishers of men" and workers in their giftings in the church. Pray that they will attend a Newcomer's Class to be prepared for the harvest of souls. *"The harvest truly is plentiful..."*[84] [_____] *"...for the people had a mind to work."*[85] [_____]

Pray for Those Responding
Pray that enough space is available in the Prayer Room after the altar call or invitation is given. *"The spirit indeed is willing, but the flesh is weak."*[86] [_____] *"Therefore pray the Lord of the harvest..."*[87] [_____] He may be calling you to pray for the harvest of souls. In the event there is an overflow in the Prayer Room, areas should be designated in advance and each person aware of the extra rooms so that there is no confusion.

It is okay to ask the person what they want prayer for. Use discernment. Ask the Lord if you are to be part of this great powerful force of His. *"Ask, and it will be given to you;"*[88] [_____] *"Yet you do not have because you do not ask."*[89] [_____] *"If any of you lacks wisdom, let him ask of God,..."*[90] [_____]

Ask the Lord for a Scripture from His Word that the person you are praying for can stand on – His promise for them right where they are. *"The entrance of Your words gives light; it gives understanding to the simple."* [91] [＿＿＿＿＿＿] *"Your kingdom come. Your will be done on earth as it is in heaven."* [92] [＿＿＿＿＿＿] *"He who has an ear, let him hear what the Spirit says to the churches."* [93] [＿＿＿＿＿＿]

Morning Prayer
Morning prayer is part of the preparation for the Prayer Room ministry. Pray for the welcoming presence of the Holy Spirit into your church during your morning prayer time. This experience starts prior to entering the Prayer Room. The morning prayer time sets the tone for the worship experience. It will be felt from the parking lot to the pulpit. It gives everyone a true sense of community.

The Lord is calling His people to the ministry of prayer. He desires to lead those with submitted and humble hearts to fulfill His will in *"Praying Your Church Into Her Glorious Destiny."* Amen. So be it!

Selah Moments (pause and meditate) – journal personal reflections from the Lord:

_____

_____

_____

_____

_____

_____

_____

_____

Section III

Praying for God's Vision

*"...that He might sanctify and cleanse her
with the washing of water by the word,
that He might present her to Himself
a glorious church, not having spot or wrinkle
or any such thing, but that she should be
holy and without blemish."*
Ephesians 5:26-27

Chapter 8

Praying for Your Visionary

Every church has an individualized fingerprint, or DNA, which equips it to fulfill God's vision for that church. It's what makes that church unique. Do you know God's vision for your church?

When you know God's vision for your church you can pray more effectively and informed. Therefore, every one of us should be able to pray in that manner.

Identify Your Visionary
It is the Senior Pastor or Bishop that has been given the vision from God for the church; they are the visionary. First, be assured that God has placed you under the Senior Pastor you have and in the church you are in. When you know you are under God's choice of pastor/visionary, you can pray with due diligence for him/her.

In the case of some churches, spouses are sharing the call of visionary as co-pastors. You will then pray for them both with thoroughness and attentiveness in the Spirit of the loving God! Do not pray carelessly for your Pastor!

Pray with Fervor
Pray with conviction for your pastor/visionary – with total abandonment for he is the one who is carrying the vision for the church! *"The effective, fervent prayer of a righteous man avails much. Elijah was a man with a nature like ours, and he prayed earnestly that it would not rain; and it did not rain on the land for three years and six*

49

months. *And he prayed again, and the heaven gave rain, and the earth produced its fruit."* [94] [_____] We call forth that level of intercessor and person of prayer who will pray with fervor for their visionary. Pray like Elijah for your visionary. He is the one God has given the mandate to prepare the church that God has given him. This kind of fervent prayer will prepare your church for *"Her Glorious Destiny."*

Praying this way is easy if you know this is God's church for you. *"And I will give you shepherds according to My heart,..."* [95] [_____]

Pray with Purity
Pray with clean hands and a pure heart for your visionary and you will be brought into covenant relationship with God and your visionary. A covenant relationship must not be tarnished with an ingratiated spirit. This will be discussed more fully in Chapter 11 – Covenant Relationship.

Pray for your visionary! Never forget – there is only one visionary: the Bishop or Senior Pastor. Be careful. Do not try to manipulate your visionary in prayer. When you don't know what to pray, simply pray that God's *"kingdom come, His will be done on earth as it is in heaven"* [96] [_____] for your visionary and your church!

Know the Body of believers the Lord has placed you in. This will cause you to pray more effectively for your church and your visionary who is leading the church. Praying for your visionary has nothing to do with whether you like him/her or not. You are mandated by

God to pray for *"...all who are in authority,..."* [97]
[_____]

I have seen people manipulate others through prayer and run to the Pastor whispering untruth. Please don't you be guilty of that sin. Do not assassinate the visionary with your tongue. The tongue has two powers: *"Death and life are in the power of the tongue,..."* [98]
[_____]

Pray with Humility
I have also seen Senior Pastors so downtrodden because of so-called know-it-all intercessors. It's like none other. I've seen and ministered to pastors hurt by these so-called intercessors and people of prayer in the churches. Tongues should be guarded, and we should speak with a spirit of love in every instance.

The intercessors are not the only ones who hear from the Lord. Allow the visionary the respect to know they hear from the Lord, too. When something is said or "a word" is delivered to him/her, it should be confirming or give them time to put it on the shelf and process whatever information they received.

Intercessors and people of prayer are not the final authority of the church. We must have respect for the spiritual authority that God has placed over us.

Pray with Purpose
Pray the Word over your visionary. Lift him/her up to always hear a Word from the Lord to feed and lead God's people. Pray that your visionary's ear is always close to the mouth of God.

Pray the Aarons and Hurs will come forth to hold up his/her hands. Pray for the spirit of helps, just as Jethro called forth for Moses, to come and assist your visionary for what God has called him/her to do!

Pray for the spirit of a Jonathan to be sent to come alongside your visionary to minister to him/her as he did for David. Pray insight to be given to the armor bearers to operate as Jonathans!

In praying for your visionary, you must also include the paid staff and volunteers. They are a type of Jonathan to your visionary.

<u>Pray Blessings</u>
Pray and speak blessings into your visionary's life; that *"...blessings shall come upon you and overtake you,"* [99]
[_____]

When you start praying blessings for your visionary, things start happening for you that you cannot explain. In praying for my visionary, I have seen the windows of heaven open on my behalf and God has poured out on me *"...such blessing that there will not be room enough to receive it."* [100] [_____]

Praying blessings for your visionary gives you peace of mind because you are walking in integrity before God. Pray blessings for him/her. *"The blessings of the Lord makes one rich, and He adds no sorrow with it."* [101]
[_____]

It is a powerful thing to pray Scriptures and release God's promises over your visionary, especially when you can personalize these prayers by inserting their name into the Scripture. Insert your visionary's name into these Scriptures:

- Prayers for Revelation:
  Ephesians 1:15-23; Colossians 1:9-14; Ephesians 3:14-19
- Prayers for Blessings:
  3 John 2-4; Deuteronomy 28:2; Numbers 6:24-26
- Prayers for Favor:
  Proverbs 13:15; Proverbs 14:35; Luke 2:52

Specific Prayers

- Pray for your visionary that God's *"will to be done on earth..."* [102] [＿＿＿＿＿＿] in his/her life as it has already been ordained in heaven by Almighty God.
- Pray for your visionary to walk in accordance with 3rd John 2, to *"prosper in all things and be in health, even as (their) soul prospers."*
- Pray for your visionary that *"the peace of God, which surpasses all understanding, will guard"* [103] [＿＿＿＿＿＿] his/her heart and mind through Christ Jesus.
- Pray for your visionary to always have the time for hearing a fresh Word from the Lord to feed you: *"And I will give you shepherds according to My heart, who will feed you with knowledge and under-standing."* [104] [＿＿＿＿＿＿]
- Pray for your visionary to be a weapon in God's hand, therefore: *"No weapon formed against (him/her) shall prosper,..."* [105] [＿＿＿＿＿＿]
- Pray for your visionary to live in joy: *"In Your presence is fullness of joy; at Your right hand are pleasures forevermore."* [106] [＿＿＿＿＿＿]
- Pray for your visionary to always have intimate time with the Lord in worship: *"...for the Father is seeking such..."* [107] [＿＿＿＿＿＿]

- Pray for your visionary and his/her family. Pray for your first lady. In the event she is a co-pastor, pray for her anyway. She is a wife also. Pray that the Lord blesses and heals them! Pray for blessings, success, and victory in their child or children's lives!

Your visionary is a gift and the one entrusted with receiving and fulfilling God's vision for your church. One of the greatest prayers for your visionary is that the church would follow him/her: follow in pursuing God's vision and follow in moving closer to *"Her Glorious Destiny."* Paul wrote to Timothy to commit the vision *"...to faithful men who will be able to teach others also."* [108] [_____] The apostles instructed the early Church to *"seek out from among you seven men of good reputation, full of the Holy Spirit and wisdom, whom we may appoint over this business; but we will give ourselves continually to prayer and to the ministry of the word."* [109] [_____]

The visionary is called to be in God's presence and receive revelation for the church. However, if the church doesn't respond and do their part, the visionary cannot do his/her part. Pray for the church to respond and the visionary to receive.

Selah Moments (pause and meditate) – journal personal reflections from the Lord:

_____

_____

_____

_____

_____

_____

_____

Chapter 9

Prayer Pastor

I realize the concept of a Prayer Pastor is new to some. Yet, I believe it is greatly needed today to pray your church into *"Her Glorious Destiny."* The Prayer Pastor is one of the two pillars to hold up the arms of the visionary – similar to Aaron and Hur holding up the arms of Moses. Moses was able to execute the things of God for the children of Israel in battle because of the assistance of Aaron and Hur. Our visionary can experience similar victories for his/her church today, with the help of a Prayer Pastor (Aaron) and an Executive Pastor (Hur).

Qualities of a Prayer Pastor
Over the past thirty-nine years of ministering in a variety of churches around the world, I have realized there is a great need within <u>some</u> churches for a Prayer Pastor. This is a position for an experienced person who has a personal covenant relationship with God and with the visionary of the church.

Qualifications should include a Kingdom mindset and a deep knowledge of spiritual authority. This person is one who would *"...seek first the kingdom of God and His righteousness,"* [110] [_____] and not the internet. Also, they should practice a life of prayer and fasting.

The Prayer Pastor should have the heart of the visionary, as well as a heart to cover the leadership of the church. Keep in mind that this is all done behind the scenes like the unseen inner structure of a building.

Praying for the Vision

The visionary cannot do it all. Help is needed to lead the church and to keep the vision before the people. *"Write the vision and make it plain on tablets, that he may run who reads it."*[111] [_____] This is where the Prayer Pastor comes in *"for the vision is yet for an appointed time; but at the end it will speak, and it will not lie."*[112] [_____] The Prayer Pastor oversees praying the vision into fruition.

What is the unique fingerprint of your church to fulfill God's vision? Who is *"making it plain?"* Who is being equipped to *"run that reads it?"* Are we preparing a generation to *"make it plain"* and *"run with it?"* There should be no confusion in the Prayer Pastors' mind of the church's vision they are called to because he/she is the one to make it plain to the intercessors and keep them focused and united.

The Prayer Pastor stewards the vision for the church through prayer, coordinating prayer assignments among the ministries of the church and the congregation.

Praying for the Visionary

The visionary should be free to prepare the Word of God and feed the people of God. The Prayer Pastor assists in leading the church and has his eyes on the things of the Spirit concerning the visionary. He/she oversees the prayer covering for the visionary and for the church.

The visionary needs help. In most cases they are apprehensive to ask. Prayer covering is absolutely necessary for the one receiving the vision from God and in spiritual authority; and the Prayer Pastor is the one who coordinates that effort. This is not a position of friendship or ingratiating with the Senior Pastor – it is one of servanthood.

Raising up Prayer Leaders
A primary function of the Prayer Pastor is to raise up prayer leaders for each ministry of the church so they have their own prayer coverage. I believe all ministries of the church should have someone to lead that area in prayer. These individuals should be equipped by the Prayer Pastor to raise up intercessors and people of prayer in their own areas of ministry. The prayer activities of these ministry prayer leaders would be coordinated and supported by the Prayer Pastor.

The Role of Aaron and Hur
The Executive Pastor leads the church in administrative and logistical functions making sure everyone is in place and the church is running up to its optimum capability.

These two positions of the Prayer Pastor and the Executive Pastor represent the Aaron and Hur for the visionary. They will also keep each other from being overly tasked. These are not sought out positions. These are positions directed by the Lord to the visionary.

Aaron and Hur each had the ear of Moses. The Prayer Pastor stands close to the visionary, being sensitive to the things of the Spirit, ministering in the "...*Spirit of wisdom and understanding, the Spirit of counsel and might,*" [113] [_____] This position is accomplished before the Lord God Almighty by fasting, intercession, and travailing on behalf of the visionary.

I realize not all churches will have these positions of a Prayer Pastor and an Executive Pastor. In the event the church does, there should be no competition between these two key positions. They both protect and cover the visionary while being led by the Holy Spirit. They offer suggestions to the visionary in line with the unique fingerprint and God's vision for their individual church.

They both know there is only one visionary directed by God. They will not seek alliance with other members of the congregation or outside the church against the visionary. Total loyalty to the visionary and God's vision for the church is a must!!!

"Praying Your Church Into Her Glorious Destiny" is accomplished by keeping *"...the unity of the Spirit in the bond of peace."* [114] [_____] Yes, *"...the kingdom of heaven suffers violence, and the violent take it by force."* [115] [_____] This is toward the enemy of the Church, Satan, and not each other. Just like the visionary cannot be everywhere, neither can the Prayer Pastor or the Executive Pastor. Your help is needed to advance the Kingdom of God.

I thank God for Prayer Pastors who are called day and night like a type of Nehemiah, building and protecting *"...so that with one hand they worked at construction, and with the other held a weapon."* [116] [_____] The enemy comes with that spirit of discouragement to bring him/her down from constructing the wall of the vision. But they will stand fast even when tested, staying on the wall to prayerfully watch over the vision. With the Prayer Pastor being a strong steward of the vision, he is helping the visionary get the job done; fulfilling God's vision and releasing the Church into *"Her Glorious Destiny."*

Selah Moments (pause and meditate) – journal personal reflections from the Lord:

_____

_____

_____

_____

_____

_____

_____

_____

Section IV

The Intercessor's Response

Search me, O God, and know my heart; test me and know my anxious thoughts.

See if there is any offensive way in me, and lead me in the way everlasting.

Psalm 139:23-24 (NIV)

Chapter 10

Intimate Relationship

My grandmother once told me, "Ask the Lord to search your heart. If not, you will misinterpret the Scripture to say what you want it to say to justify your actions. You will see and hear the truth and call it a lie." *"Be diligent to present yourself approved to God, a worker who does not need to be ashamed, rightly dividing the word of truth."* [117] [_____]

The Fruit of an Intimate Relationship

Taking time to read the Word, pray, fast, and worship the Lord will build godly character. Operate in a spirit of excellence and obedience knowing *"to obey is better than sacrifice."* [118] [_____]

Always be faithful to seek His face and not His hands. In other words, intimate relationship with the Lord will keep you from constantly begging. It brings you to the level of confidence knowing whatever you ask in His name and according to His will, He will grant you.

Intimate relationship with the Lord can build your self-esteem. *"When my heart is overwhelmed; lead me to the rock that is higher than I."* [119] [_____]

Intimate relationship will cause you to walk with a repentant heart. I cannot tell you the number of times I cry out to Him for help. No, our intimate relationship with the Lord will not keep us from sometimes feeling sad or hoping we could circumvent trouble or sickness. It does, however, cause me to run to the Lord; to call upon Him. It causes me to be compassionate to others.

And His love for me allows me to love others *"for love will cover a multitude of sins."* [120] [_____]

When you have an intimate relationship with God, it is evident you are easily entreated. One is *"...a sweet smelling aroma."* [121] [_____] In other words, it is the condition of your heart. The Lord promises *"...you will seek Me and find Me, when you search for Me with all your heart."* [122] [_____]

You are more apt to stay prostrate before Him in a spirit of waiting on the Lord. You know He loves you. You know *"...those who wait on the LORD shall renew their strength;..."* [123] [_____]

When that intimate relationship is in place with the King of kings and the Lord of lords, you have *"...a broken and contrite heart,..."* [124] [_____] You are the one to say it is *"Not by might nor by power, but by My Spirit, says the LORD of hosts"* [125] [_____] that things are done! Everything you do is through a spirit of love knowing it *"...will cover a multitude of sins."* [126] [_____]

Intimacy Through Consecration
I have overcome numerous adversities through prayer and fasting. Things of the flesh are removed from the Church, as well as from individuals who live a consecrated life. And it is a consecrated life that has created more room for the life of Christ to dwell – producing greater intimacy with Him.

A life of fasting and consecration before the Lord was a way of life for my grandmother. Now, after all these years, I find myself praying the same prayers she has

prayed: *"Purge me with hyssop, and I shall be clean; wash me, and I shall be whiter than snow."* [127] [_____]
"Hide Your face from my sins, and blot out all my iniquities." [128] [_____] *"Then I will teach transgressors Your ways, and sinners shall be converted to You."* [129] [_____]

You cannot be an intercessor and be moody. Consecration takes care of all of that. I recall once the Lord told me, "Amelda, I have not called you to lock yourself away from people. You do that because you do not want to have anything to do with them."

I am a runner, one who will hide and stay by myself. The devil knows that. That is when the Holy Ghost will enter my consecrated heart. He will step in knowing I'm weak. He will whisper to me in that *"...still small voice"* [130] [_____]; encouraging fellowship and *"not forsaking the assembling of ourselves together..."* [131] [_____] His strength comes through the reassurance that He *"...is able to keep you from stumbling, and present you faultless before the presence of His Glory..."* [132] [_____]; *"...Who alone is wise,..."* [133] [_____]

Intimacy Through Repentance
Intercessors and people of prayer must lead a life of repentance to experience intimacy with the Lord. I have had several defining moments when the Lord God Almighty had to bring me up before Him in a spirit of repentance. That is what an intimate relationship with Him will do for you. That is what a consecrated life will bring you. Waiting in His presence will remove the dross from you!

To build an intimate relationship with the Lord, study Psalm 51. Highlight the verses that speak to you and have the Holy Spirit come with a time of refreshing to heal you. I have done this and it has brought me the balm of Gilead to heal me from sins, disappointments, and the hurts of man. He will do the same for you. I still practice Selah moments of this Psalms. This is a start; you also will find the Word that will bring you the healing and soothing balm! For each of us there will come a time when we will say to the Lord:

"Have mercy upon me, O God, according to Your lovingkindness; according to the multitude of Your tender mercies, blot out my transgressions. Wash me thoroughly from my iniquity, and cleanse me from my sin." (Psalm 51:1-2)

If you have not experienced this yet - live long enough and you will cry out:

"For I acknowledge my transgressions, and my sin is always before me." (Psalm 51:3)

Knowing it is against Him alone you have sinned:

"Against You, You only, have I sinned, and done this evil in Your sight — that You may be found just when You speak, and blameless when You judge. Behold, I was brought forth in iniquity, and in sin my mother conceived me. Behold, You desire truth in the inward parts, and in the hidden part You will make me to know wisdom." (Psalm 51:4-6)

Your cry for spiritual cleansing will come from the Lord:

"Purge me with hyssop, and I shall be clean; Wash me, and I shall be whiter than snow. Make me hear joy and gladness, that the bones You have broken may rejoice.

Hide Your face from my sins, and blot out all my iniquities." (Psalm 51:7-9)

I cannot tell you how many times I have had to say:
"Create in me a clean heart, O God, and renew a steadfast spirit within me. Do not cast me away from Your presence, and do not take Your Holy Spirit from me. Restore to me the joy of Your salvation, and uphold me by Your generous Spirit. Then I will teach transgressors Your ways, and sinners shall be converted to You." (Psalm 51:10-13)

In my hurt and wanting revenge, I have had to remember there is purpose and destiny on my life. Then I had to say:
"Deliver me from the guilt of bloodshed, O God, the God of my salvation, and my tongue shall sing aloud of Your righteousness. O Lord, open my lips, and my mouth shall show forth Your praise. For You do not desire sacrifice, or else I would give it; You do not delight in burnt offering. The sacrifices of God are a broken spirit, a broken and a contrite heart — these, O God, You will not despise. Do good in Your good pleasure to Zion; build the walls of Jerusalem. Then You shall be pleased with the sacrifices of righteousness, with burnt offering and whole burnt offering; then they shall offer bulls on Your altar." (Psalm 51:14-19)

Intimacy Through Fasting

Do not think fasting and dieting are the same. It does not work. The fasting I am talking about is the one Jesus completed before His ministry started. Be prepared. With that type of fast, the first thing you will encounter is the devil. He will use the Word like he did with Jesus.

Be prepared to respond like Jesus did. He used the Word. Jesus was and still is the Word. Stay in and connected to the Word. Jesus is the Word you will remain connected with. *"I am the true vine, and My Father is the vinedresser."* [134] [_____]

There are various fasts described throughout the Bible. Choose the one that best suits you. The one you choose is left up to you and the Lord. No matter which one you choose, if you follow its precepts, then you will have success. In my opinion, there are two types of fasts: one that pleases the flesh; and one that pleases God. Which fast will you choose? The fast that pleases man is Isaiah 58:2-5; the fast that pleases God is Isaiah 58:6-12.

I have experienced both types of fasts. Yet the fasting that pleases God is the one that brought me peace of mind, something money or possessions cannot give. In pleasing God, you can pray the Church into *"Her Glorious Destiny"* unencumbered.

You are the Church He will cleanse and sanctify because He loves you. He is making us holy because *"...it is written, 'Be holy, for I am holy.'"* [135] [_____] We become holy only through repentance and consecration; and this is the pathway to intimacy. God so desires His people to know Him intimately so they will pray His heart.

Know that it is not the abundance of words you pray that validates your prayer before God, nor your tone of voice. It is through the condition of the heart or sincerity of your heart that your mouth will speak. *"For out of the abundance of the heart his mouth speaks."* [136] [_____] Keep in mind that *"man looks at the*

outward appearance, but the Lord looks at the heart." [137]
[_____]

The Lord reveals His heart to those in intimate relationship with Him. The closer and more intimate we become, the more He reveals of Himself. It is through consecration, repentance, and fasting that we *"Draw near to God and He will draw near to you."* [138] [_____] It is out of this place of nearness with the Lord comes the intimate prayers like David prayed: Holy Father, *"As the deer pants for the water brooks, so pants my soul for You, O God."* [139] [_____] *"In Your presence is fullness of joy; at Your right hand are pleasures forevermore."* [140] [_____]

Invest in your intimate relationship with the Lord; it has eternal rewards.

Selah Moments (pause and meditate) – journal personal reflections from the Lord:

_____
_____
_____
_____
_____
_____
_____
_____

Chapter 11

Covenant Relationship

We serve a covenant keeping God. If we are to fulfill our calling to pray the Church into *"Her Glorious Destiny,"* we need to understand and enter into a covenant relationship with Him. We must also pass down these covenant principles to the generations to come so they, too, can fulfill their call to pray forth God's vision.

A covenant is an agreement between you and another. According to the Thesaurus, covenant means: Agreement; Contract; Treaty; Promise; Pledge; between two or more parties.

The covenant relationship with God and the visionary of your church will bring you into harmony with your Creator and His vision for your church. Ask the Father to reveal to you the matriarch or patriarch from Scripture that best exemplifies your covenant relationship with Him and with your church. He will. *"Ask, and it will be given to you;"* [141] [_____]

Abraham's Example
The Lord gave me Abraham as an example of covenant relationship because of my own shortcomings. Yet, His love has redeemed me so I could leave this book as a legacy.

Abraham's covenant relationship with God was imperative for him in becoming the *"father of many nations."* The generations need to know the forgiveness and love of God through covenant relationship so they, too, can pray the Church into *"Her Glorious Destiny."*

The story of Abraham illustrates God's dedication to him through their covenant relationship. In spite of lying about Sarah being his sister and sleeping with Hagar, God forgave him and used him mightily. He will use you also! Let Him.

Abraham's Faith
Abraham had complete confidence in God through his covenant relationship with Him. He obeyed God and took Isaac to Mount Moriah and knew God as Jehovah, his Provider. God saved Abraham's family member, Lot, and he knew God to be *"...mighty to save."*[142] [_____] It was through trust in God and obedience to Him that Abraham became *"...fully convinced that what He had promised He was also able to perform."*[143] [_____] And Abraham's faith in his covenant partner, God Himself, was *"...accounted to him for righteousness."*[144] [_____]

Covenant with God
Covenant is established through relationship. The first covenant relationship is with God, then with each other. Our covenant with God is indefinite. He will never break His covenant or relationship with us. We are the ones who will walk away from Him. Yet, if we will repent and *"...confess our sins, He is faithful and just to forgive us our sins and to cleanse us from all unrighteousness."*[145] [_____]

Each of us should have the peace of God in our relationship with the Lord and each other. It is only through the covenant we have with God that we can experience a successful and victorious covenant with each other.

Covenant with Others
Our covenant with each other should operate similarly to the one we have with God. We must forgive *"...one another, even as God in Christ forgave you."* [146] [   ] In covenant relationship we can agree to disagree, without being disrespectful and stop speaking to each other. When in disagreement, be open to come together so that an offense will not occur and split the relationship.

Some agreements between each other are seasonal. *"To everything there is a season,"* [147] [   ] Now the type of covenant you enter into can be for a period of time, or it can be indefinite. However, this should be agreed to between all those concerned.

God's Promises and Provision
Abraham's journey with God was a wonderful one - so should our journey be with God. God provided for him because of his obedience. Two things God gave to Abraham even with his shortcomings: His promises and His provision. What God did for Abraham, He will do for you and me. You can be a recipient of His grace just like Abraham. God has "promises and provision" for you. Jesus paid your price on the Cross. Thank God for His grace! He will cut a covenant with you. And as you covenant with others, His promises are yes and amen!

Walk in covenant integrity. That is doing the right thing when you think no one is looking. Keep in mind God sees, hears, and knows everything you are doing! Abraham was found faithful in his covenant relationship

with God and man. He received the promise. *"By faith Abraham obeyed when he was called to go out to the place which he would receive as an inheritance."*[148]
[_____]

Through my covenant relationship with God and others, I have been empowered to experience His promises and provision, in the true sense of the word. You can also; God is no respecter of persons. With a broken and contrite heart before God, we can also receive His promises and be sustained by His provision.

It is through our covenant relationship with God and each other that we begin to experience the promise of Jesus' heart – a Bride not having spot or wrinkle, holy and without blemish – a church living and moving closer and closer to *"Her Glorious Destiny."*

Selah Moments (pause and meditate) – journal personal reflections from the Lord:

_____

_____

_____

_____

_____

_____

_____

Chapter 12

Who the Bible Says I Am

I cannot tell you the amount of times as a teenager my grandmother told me to get my self-worth from the Lord. She would say to me, "Amelda, go and search the Word and tell me who the Lord says you are." I have done this with my own children. Try it for yourself. Today, I continue to find who I am in Him. Find out who you are in Him.

When I found the word "BELOVED" in the Bible, I fell in love for the first time in my life. You, too, are His beloved; receive His affection for you:

- *"The **beloved** of the LORD shall dwell in safety by Him."* [149] [_____]
- *"For so He gives His **beloved** sleep."* [150] [_____]
- *"At the beginning of your supplications the command went out, and I have come to tell you, for you are greatly **beloved**:"* [151] [_____]
- *"This is My **beloved** Son, in whom I am well pleased."* [152] [_____]
- *"He made us accepted in the **Beloved**."* [153] [_____]
- *"I am my **beloved's**, and my **beloved** is mine."* [154] [_____]
- *"**Beloved**, I pray that you may prosper in all things and be in health, just as your soul prospers."* [155] [_____]

The Bible has so much to say about who we are in Christ. Gaining our identity from Christ is especially valuable for those who have had the tendency to be a "man pleaser." A "man pleaser" is one who seeks their self-worth from mankind, or one who makes wrong decisions, or gets involved with the wrong people in order to be affirmed. Beloved, you are already accepted in the Beloved.

Get your identity and affirmation from the Lord. Men will deceive you! Those of us who get our identity from Him will not fight identity depression or suffer from low self-esteem!

Who the Lord says that I am is answered in His Word, the Bible. This is what I choose to base my identity. If you are like me, you want to know what the Bible has to say about who I am:

- **I am** a child of God: *"But as many as received Him, to them He gave the right to become children of God,"* [156] [_____]
- **I am** a friend of Jesus Christ: He said, *"...I have called you friends,"* [157] [_____]
- **I am** a *"...treasure in earthen vessels."* [158] [_____]
- **I am** a *"...pearl of great price,"* [159] [_____]
- **I am** the Lord's: *"...do you not know...you are not your own? For you were bought at a price."* [160] [_____]
- **I am** a *"...royal priesthood,"* [161] [_____]
- **I am** a member of Christ's body: *"Now you are the body of Christ, and members individually."* [162] [_____]
- **I am** redeemed and forgiven of all my sins: *"He has delivered us from the power of darkness and conveyed us into the kingdom of the Son of His love, in whom we have redemption through His blood, the forgiveness of sins."* [163] [_____]

76

- **I am** made in the image of God: *"Then God said, 'Let Us make man in Our image, according to Our likeness; let them have dominion over the fish of the sea, over the birds of the air, and over the cattle, over all the earth and over every creeping thing that creeps on the earth.' So God created man in His own image; in the image of God He created him; male and female He created them."* [164] [＿＿＿＿＿＿]
- **I am** complete in Christ: *"...you are complete in Him, who is the head of all principality and power."* [165] [＿＿＿＿＿＿]

Beloved, I would like to take this opportunity and encourage you in your most holy faith. Build yourself up praying in the Spirit. Take the Scriptural nuggets the Lord has had me share with you as a building block. This is all about you and who God says you are. Now build upon it. This foundational interaction between you and the Father is of the utmost importance. It is all in reference to how you see yourself: who you are and Whose you are.

Please know you are the Lord's *"...pearl of great price."* [166] [＿＿＿＿＿＿] He sold everything by giving up His life to purchase you. You are that important to Him. You are now accepted into the Beloved! Receive and live this truth – for His glory and for your glorious destiny as part of His Bride, the Church. Amen!

Selah Moments (pause and meditate) – journal personal reflections from the Lord:

_____

_____

_____

_____

_____

_____

_____

_____

Chapter 13

Spiritual Food to Remember

Power in the Name of Jesus

For everything there is a season. This is the season of empowering ourselves in Jesus' name through the Word of God. This will enable us to stand in these last and evil days. *"Your word I have hidden in my heart, that I might not sin against You."*[167] [＿＿＿＿＿＿]

God help us if we are found to be powerless. The sons of Sceva tried to use the name of Jesus without the power. The demons knew they did not know what they were talking about. As you are *"Praying Your Church Into Her Glorious Destiny,"* pray with power so you don't end up like the sons of Sceva: *"Jesus I know, and Paul I know; but who are you?"*[168] [＿＿＿＿＿＿]

The only way we can know the power in the name of Jesus is to nurture ourselves with the spiritual food of His Word. Let us grow *"...from glory to glory, just as by the Spirit of the Lord."*[169] [＿＿＿＿＿＿] *"And let us not grow weary while doing good,"*[170] [＿＿＿＿＿＿] This is achieved by eating and meditating on God's Word on a continuous basis; being *"...diligent to present yourself approved to God,...rightly dividing the word of truth."*[171] [＿＿＿＿＿＿]

The Bible says: *"The name of the LORD is a strong tower; the righteous run to it and are safe."*[172] [＿＿＿＿＿＿] There is power at the mention of the name of Jesus: *"...that at the name of Jesus every knee should bow,...and that every tongue should confess that Jesus Christ is Lord,"*[173] [＿＿＿＿＿＿]

We must have and maintain an intimate relationship with the Lord. In the natural we eat three times a day, and we snack just as often. The same is true with our relationship with the Lord. In order for us to know and experience the power in the name of Jesus, we must be feeding ourselves with the food of God's Word.

Pray in the Name of Jesus

"And in that day you will ask Me nothing. Most assuredly, I say to you, whatever you ask the Father in My name He will give you." [174] [_____] Jesus said for us to pray to the Father in His name and He would do whatever we ask. This promise is tied to Jesus' confession in the Garden when He prayed, *"...take this cup away from Me; nevertheless not My will, but Yours, be done."* [175] [_____] The power to receive our answer to prayer is found in praying according to the will and Word of God.

Ministry of the Holy Spirit

Jesus promised that *"...you shall receive power when the Holy Spirit has come upon you; and you shall be witnesses to Me..."* [176] [_____] And it is the Holy Spirit who *"...will teach you all things and will remind you of everything I have said to you,"* [177] [_____] It is also the Holy Spirit who *"...will guide you into all truth,"* [178] [_____] Know that you know that God is able to keep you *"...from stumbling, and to present you faultless before the presence of His glory with exceeding joy."* [179] [_____]

Never Stop Contending

Because of our spiritual nourishment in the Word of God and our intimate relationship with Jesus, we are able to: experience power in His name; confidently pray in His name; and release the ministry of the Holy Spirit. We are now equipped to pray our church into *"Her Glorious Destiny."*

Keep in mind as you pray, the Lord has three possible answers: yes, no, or wait. "Yes" will bring Him glory as you show and testify to His glory. When He says "no" to your request, you know from your spiritual nutrition in His Word that He has something better for you. I have experienced this for myself and I know from experience. In waiting on the Lord, we are guaranteed He will not leave us comfortless during our time of waiting.

Maintain your life with God by *"...building yourselves up on your most holy faith, praying in the Holy Spirit, keep yourselves in the love of God, looking for the mercy of our Lord Jesus Christ unto eternal life."* [180] [   ]

Knowing what I know, I must impart prayer into the Church. I must impart prayer into you, this generation, and generations to come - it's my destiny. It's non-negotiable. I will teach should the Lord tarry. This is my mandate from the Lord: to equip you in *"Praying Your Church Into Her Glorious Destiny."* In Jesus' name.

Selah Moments (pause and meditate) – journal personal reflections from the Lord:

_____

_____

_____

_____

_____

_____

_____

Appendix

Chapter 1:
[1] 1 Thessalonians 5:17
[2] Matthew 16:18
[3] Luke 18:1
[4] Jeremiah 17:9
[5] Acts 17:28
[6] Malachi 3:10
[7] 2 Corinthians 9:7
[8] 1 Corinthians 14:40
[9] James 5:16
[10] 2 Timothy 2:15
[11] Matthew 18:20
[12] Jude 3
[13] John 14:13
[14] John 13:34
[15] Luke 11:2

Chapter 2:
[16] Ephesians 5:27
[17] John 16:13
[18] Philippians 4:6
[19] 1 Samuel 30:8
[20] 1 Samuel 30:8
[21] Numbers 23:19
[22] Jeremiah 29:13
[23] 1 Timothy 2:8
[24] Ezekiel 22:30
[25] 1 Timothy 2:1-2
[26] 2 Chronicles 7:14

Chapter 3:
[27] Hebrews 12:2
[28] Ephesians 4:32
[29] Psalm 24:4
[30] 1 Samuel 16:7
[31] Galatians 6:7
[32] Ephesians 4:32
[33] Matthew 18:8
[34] Matthew 18:11
[35] Matthew 18:20

[36] Hebrews 7:25
[37] Matthew 15:14
[38] 2 Peter 1:10

Chapter 4:
[39] Hebrews 7:25
[40] Ezekiel 22:30
[41] Proverbs 18:16
[42] Psalm 24:4
[43] Luke 22:26
[44] Matthew 18:15
[45] Matthew 18:16
[46] Ephesians 4:32
[47] Ephesians 4:3
[48] Ephesians 5:26-27
[49] 1 Peter 1:16
[50] Ephesians 6:12
[51] 1 John 1:7
[52] Ephesians 6:11
[53] Jude 3
[54] Matthew 10:19-20
[55] Romans 12:10
[56] Matthew 6:6
[57] Psalm 91:5

Chapter 5:
[58] 1 John 4:19
[59] Isaiah 55:11
[60] Colossians 1:10
[61] Hebrews 3:15
[62] John 8:32
[63] John 8:36
[64] Ephesians 2:16
[65] Matthew 6:10
[66] Mark 16:17
[67] 1 John 5:14-15

Chapter 6:
[68] Psalm 139:23
[69] Psalm 24:4
[70] Hebrews 13:5

Chapter 7:
[71] Revelation 2:7
[72] Psalm 119:105
[73] Jeremiah 31:3
[74] John 4:23
[75] 1 Chronicles 16:29
[76] 2 Corinthians 9:7
[77] Isaiah 55:11
[78] Psalm 119:105
[79] Psalm 119:11
[80] Psalm 119:130
[81] 2 Corinthians 2:4-5
[82] Revelation 3:20
[83] Acts 1:8
[84] Matthew 9:37
[85] Nehemiah 4:6
[86] Matthew 26:41
[87] Matthew 9:37
[88] Matthew 7:7
[89] James 4:2
[90] James 1:5
[91] Psalm 119:130
[92] Matthew 6:10
[93] Revelation 2:7

Chapter 8:
[94] James 5:16-18
[95] Jeremiah 3:15
[96] Matthew 6:10
[97] 1 Timothy 2:1-2
[98] Proverbs 18:21
[99] Deuteronomy 28:2
[100] Malachi 3:10
[101] Proverbs 10:22
[102] Matthew 6:10
[103] Philippians 4:7
[104] Jeremiah 3:15
[105] Isaiah 54:17
[106] Psalm 16:11

[107] John 4:23
[108] 2 Timothy 2:2
[109] Acts 6:3-4

Chapter 9:
[110] Matthew 6:33
[111] Habakkuk 2:2
[112] Habakkuk 2:3
[113] Isaiah 11:2
[114] Ephesians 4:3
[115] Matthew 11:12
[116] Nehemiah 4:17

Chapter 10:
[117] 2 Timothy 2:15
[118] 1 Samuel 15:22
[119] Psalm 61:2
[120] 1 Peter 4:8
[121] Ephesians 5:2
[122] Jeremiah 29:13
[123] Isaiah 40:31
[124] Psalm 51:17
[125] Zechariah 4:6
[126] 1 Peter 4:8
[127] Psalm 51:7
[128] Psalm 51:9
[129] Psalm 51:13
[130] 1 Kings 19:12
[131] Hebrews 10:25

[132] Jude 24
[133] Jude 25
[134] John 15:1
[135] 1 Peter 1:16
[136] Luke 6:45
[137] 1 Samuel 16:7
[138] James 4:8
[139] Psalm 42:1
[140] Psalm 16:11

Chapter 11:
[141] Matthew 7:7
[142] Isaiah 63:1
[143] Romans 4:21
[144] Romans 4:22
[145] 1 John 1:9
[146] Ephesians 4:32
[147] Ecclesiastes 3:1
[148] Hebrews 11:8

Chapter 12:
[149] Deuteronomy 33:12
[150] Psalm 127:2
[151] Daniel 9:23
[152] Matthew 3:17
[153] Ephesians 1:6
[154] Song of Solomon 6:3
[155] 3 John 2

[156] John 1:12
[157] John 15:15
[158] 2 Corinthians 4:7
[159] Matthew 13:46
[160] I Corinthians 6:19-20
[161] 1 Peter 2:9
[162] 1 Corinthians 12:27
[163] Colossians 1:13-14
[164] Genesis 1:26-27
[165] Colossians 2:10
[166] Matthew 13:46

Chapter 13:
[167] Psalm 119:11
[168] Acts 19:15
[169] 2 Corinthians 3:18
[170] Galatians 6:9
[171] 2 Timothy 2:15
[172] Proverbs 18:10
[173] Philippians 2:10-11
[174] John 16:23
[175] Luke 22:43
[176] Acts 1:8
[177] John 14:26
[178] John 16:13
[179] Jude 24
[180] Jude 20

"COVENANT"

"Praying Your Church Into Her Glorious Destiny"

This COVENANT is a covenant with your church, organization, ministry and/or person in *"Praying Your Church Into Her Glorious Destiny"* as an intercessor or person of prayer.

Let it be known, this book covers the various areas you will be expected to covenant in. You are further expected to search the Scriptures, under the leading of the Holy Spirit, to find the covenant God made with a Biblical character that best describes you. Fill in the blanks below:

        Character Name: _____

        Scriptural Reference: _____

Remember, a covenant is an agreement and a promise between you and another! Should you decide to break it, follow the same protocol as initiating it – walking in integrity!

- - - - - - - - - - - - - - - - - - -Tear along line and turn in - - - - - - - - - - - - - - - - - -

---

Organization that I am entering into covenant with:

_____

Print your name: _____

Your signature: _____

Date: _____

Yes, I will serve: _____ No, I will not serve: _____